by Susan Bierko
illustrated by Celine Malepart

SCHOOL PUBLISHERS

Printed in China

ISBN 10: 0-15-350002-6
ISBN 13: 978-0-15-350002-2

Ordering Options
ISBN 10: 0-15-349938-9 (Grade 3 ELL Collection)
ISBN 13: 978-0-15-349938-8 (Grade 3 ELL Collection)
ISBN 10: 0-15-357241-8 (package of 5)
ISBN 13: 978-0-15-357241-8 (package of 5)

1 2 3 4 5 6 7 8 9 10 985 12 11 10 09 08 07 06

Javier looks across the field. He sees Frankie and waves. Frankie waves back. He runs over to say hello to Javier. Javier whispers something. Frankie laughs. Then Javier laughs. They are friends.

Sonia and Rosa sit next to each other in school. They play together at recess. They sit next to each other on the school bus. They are friends, too.

Sometimes it is easy to make friends. Sara and Carl live next to each othcr. They go to school together. They play together. Their families spend time together.

Sometimes you have to try hard to make friends. Alex's family moved to a new town. He did not know anyone in his new school. He felt worried on the first day.

Then the teacher introduced Alex to the class. She showed him his desk.

The boy next to Alex smiled a pleasant smile. The boy's name was Sam. He showed Alex the page in the book.

They found out that they both liked cars. Sam and Alex both liked to draw, too.

Sometimes friends like different things. Leah likes to work on her computer. Sandra always wants to play outside. Leah likes to sing in front of people. Sandra is very shy. Sandra and Leah still have fun together.

They have tried new things because of each other. Leah learned to play soccer. Sandra wrote a story on the computer. Sandra even sang a song with Leah at a school concert!

Robbie was sure he was going to win the race. He tripped near the finish line. He did not win. Robbie's friend Jamie helped him up. He asked Robbie whether he was hurt. Robbie felt better.

Loyal friends support each other. They listen and help.

Trina's class was having a pool party. Trina did not know how to swim. She did not want to go to the party. Trina's best friend, Laura, asked her to go anyway.

Laura was a good swimmer. She spent most of the day outside the water with Trina. They talked and played games. They had fun. Other children asked Laura why Trina did not go in the water.

Laura told them that she and Trina were having fun doing other things. Laura knew Trina did not want people to know she could not swim.

Friends tell each other secrets. Then they trust each other to keep their secrets.

What is a friend? A friend is a special person in your life. You can have fun with a friend. You can trust a friend. A friend shares happy times. A friend helps you.

Best Friends!

Scaffolded Language Development

To the Teacher

CONCEPT WORDS Ask students what some things are that friends do for one another. Suggest that students think about things that they could do for their friends. Model by saying something that you could do for a friend. For example, you might help a friend pick up a mess. Then, have students use the word bank to complete the sentences below. Have them say the completed sentences chorally.

Word Bank: play, together, help, talk

1. Friends _____ games with each other.

2. Friends do things _____.

3. Friends _____ each other solve problems.

4. Friends _____ to each other.

 ## Social Studies

Friends Are Everywhere Have students pretend that they moved to a new town like Alex did in the book. Talk with students about some ways they could make friends in a new community. Help students generate a list of ideas to share with students who may be new to their community in the future.

 ## School-Home Connection
Old and New Friends Ask students to talk about friends with family members. Some topics for discussion could be what family members enjoy doing with friends and how they became friends.

Word Count: 430